AMAZON REVIEWS *for* BOOKS

HOW TO GET BOOK REVIEWS ON AMAZON

THE AMAZON SELF PUBLISHER SERIES, BOOK 3

DALE L. ROBERTS

Amazon Reviews for Books: How to Get Book Reviews on Amazon

By Dale L. Roberts

©2020 One Jacked Monkey, LLC

Amazon is a registered trademark of Amazon.com, Inc. This book is not authorized or endorsed by Amazon.com, Inc.

Some recommended links in this book are part of affiliate programs. This means if you purchase a product through one of the links, then I get a portion of each sale. It doesn't affect your cost and greatly helps support the cause. If you have any reservations about buying a product through my affiliate link, then feel free to Google a direct link and bypass the affiliate link.

Cover design by MaMarko78 on Fiverr. To see his services, visit: https://dalelinks.com/coversbymarko.

Find out how I found Marko and why I selected him for cover design services in the video at https://dalelinks.com/5designs.

Interior design and typesetting by Archangel Ink at ArchangelInk.com.

ISBN: 978-1-950043-18-7

Are you ready to begin your own self-publishing journey?
You have a story.
It deserves to be told.

Learn the fundamentals of self-publishing books…

In this in-depth, yet succinct, course.

The DIY Publishing Course for Beginners

It's perfect for anyone new to the self-publishing business!
It will take you from manuscript to self-published.

The best part? It's 100% free!

Visit DIYPublishing.biz/Free to enroll today.

Contents

*A*fter six years of being in self-publishing, it was high time I shared insights about getting more book reviews. Though I ran a YouTube channel and built a brand around *Self-Publishing with Dale*, I didn't have any books covering the art of self-publishing. Why? Between publishing a fitness brand and maintaining my YouTube brand, life just got in the way.

It was only a matter of time before I finally pivoted away from fitness publishing and shared insights into the world of self-publishing. A few months ago, I broke ground in the *Amazon Self-Publisher Series* with *Amazon Keywords for Books*. Shortly after that, I released the second part, *Promotional Strategies for Books*. Now we come to the final part of the series in *Amazon Reviews for Books*.

The Amazon Self-Publisher Series focuses on the most common pain points authors and self-publishers have in using the Amazon platform:

1. Keywords

2. Marketing and promotion

3. Reviews

Though you could Google your way around and find all the answers you need, the real issue you run into is time. Do you really want to waste your time trying to piece together what is right or wrong? Would you know fact from fiction? What if I could set you up with everything you need without all the hassle? Imagine cutting out all the noise and focusing on precisely what you need to know now to move your author career forward.

Enter *The Amazon Self-Publisher Series*.

Amazon Reviews for Books: How to Get Book Reviews on Amazon is the perfect finale for this three-part series. Once you read the entire series, you'll have what you need to handle the biggest issues plaguing self-publishers using the Amazon platform.

Dig in and happy publishing!

–Dale L. Roberts

I love tacos. There's no way around it. I tried everything I could to avoid eating tacos. Inevitably, my life guides me toward the nearest taco vendor. Any old taco will not do. I need some assurance the tacos are of premium quality and not some low-grade stuff. Price isn't the issue so much as how good the food is and the value of the service. Naturally, I'll dig out my phone and look up reviews on the establishment. I'm always drawn to the low one-star reviews and tend to scan past the high marks and praise in the five-star reviews. I want to see the complaints. It's easy to give a restaurant, service, or product a high review. It's the low reviews that tell a better story.

When I first moved to downtown Columbus, I visited the Condado Tacos restaurant around the corner from my place. I whipped out Yelp, scanned through the low reviews, and found some rather innocuous complaints about lousy service and improper food serving. Beyond that, it seemed good to go. Little did I know that I'd spend thousands of dollars and countless hours visiting this restaurant. To say I'm a fan is a huge understatement. Between birthdays and business meetings, I've done just about everything there is to do at Condado Tacos.

Naturally, any time someone comes into town, I take them to Condado Tacos. If I have a business meeting, then I take them to Condado Tacos. When my wife and I need to get out of the house, we go to Condado Tacos. My enthusiasm for the restaurant spilled so far out of my life;

3

I've seen friends and family even visit when I'm not with them. That speaks volumes about how excellent their service is.

Of course, I left beaming reviews on Yelp and Google. I've checked in through the Yelp app, snapped some pictures, and tagged some friends. In turn, all the people I brought to the establishment did the same. They brought in more friends who became hooked. All those people then left great reviews. I'm sure it had a massive ripple effect throughout the whole Columbus-area.

It all started with reviews. Had I not seen a review about the establishment, I would've been less likely to go in. After all, there's a Chipotle – the McDonald's of Mexican food - not even a mile down the road. I didn't want to experience the same ol' tired taco fanfare. I wanted something a bit different on that given day, and I was not disappointed.

Imagine how different life would be had I not seen some type of social proof. Would I skip the restaurant without some validation? Would I go to Chipotle, where they have countless reviews? Would I be brave enough to give it a shot and try it out? Would the other people who came with me try out the place? Would the people who would have seen my review passed on those tasty tacos? These are what-if scenarios we won't truly know.

The fact is we're in a day and age where social proof is almost a necessity. To cut through the noise, be heard above the pack, and stand out from the rest, we need someone to lend third-party credibility. It's that stamp of approval, or sometimes disapproval, we need to show we have something worth considering.

Self-publishing can be a dark, hard, and lonely road as it is. To make matters worse, we cannot even begin to gain traction without someone saying, "Hey, this author's alright."

Sometimes, it's not enough to even get one person saying it. It's not even a given number of people saying it. We need a consistent stream of social proof to earn the trust of a potential reader. Where one review posted in 2015 was good five years ago, it doesn't speak to your product's relevance today.

In this book, we're going to focus on how to get reviews, what to do with them, and how getting reviews are an integral part of your marketing and promotional strategy. Keep in mind, as you push through this book, some concepts are going to seem rudimentary. Hang in there because I'm laying a foundation of things to come. You must learn how to crawl before you can walk or even begin to run.

Once you finish this book, you'll have enough advice and practical steps to build more relevancy on your books with a consistent flow of reviews on the Amazon platform. I want to see you succeed beyond measure, and the best way to do that is to load you up with sensible advice. Put down your tacos, wipe off your fingers, and let's dig right into how to get more book reviews on Amazon.

Reviews play an integral part in the development and exposure of your book and brand. Having a review is the validation of someone experiencing your product on the Amazon marketplace. Can you still sell books without reviews? Absolutely, but you start at a greater disadvantage than other books like yours with reviews.

For instance, a customer searches for a book in their favorite genre, werebear shapeshifter romance. Amazon serves the first sixteen options on the first-page query results. In this example, one book has no reviews, while the other book has seventy-two reviews. Both covers look great. The titles seem interesting. Heck, even the book description is compelling, but the differentiating factor is the customer has one book with reviews while the other has none. Does the customer take a chance and buy a book without any social proof, or do they go with the crowd and buy the book with seventy-two reviews?

> *Nothing attracts a crowd like a crowd.*

People love to share the same experience with other people, especially if it's great. There's a sense of community built around an experience, whether it's a great restaurant or a good book. When people enjoy something, they want to pass that experience to other people. Conversely, when the experience is unpleasant, they're quick to urge people away from it. Each instance tells a different story and plays an integral role in other people wanting to take part.

For instance, I'm always rubbernecking in the low end of the reviews pool. Why? I get an honest look at what went wrong in the experience. When the experience is unsatisfactory, I'm curious as to why. Will my opinion vary from the reviewer, or will I agree with them?

Ultimately, reviews on Amazon play a vital role in customers making an informed purchase. Though a fraction of customers probably know what they want and skip the reviews, a large majority will skim through the reviews to see if it's a good fit. Where some authors get it wrong is the low reviews. While it sucks to hear someone trashing your book, that review reveals a bigger picture. In some cases, that low review entices a different mindset or customer to purchase it.

Here's the deal with reviews. When a customer visits your product page, they either pass, or they buy. There's no middle of the road. They have two choices and one decision to make. If the browsing customer buys, then you increase your conversion rate. What are you converting? Browsing customers into buyers. The more customers you convert, the more Amazon rewards your product page with additional traffic. The lower the conversion rate, the less traffic Amazon sends.

At the end of the day, Amazon wants to make money. If you're in it to do the same thing, then Amazon will be in your court. However, suppose you're not in it to make money or convert more customers into buyers. In that case, Amazon will move onto other authors who do align with their goal. Higher conversion rates increase your rankings in the search results, leading to more discoverability. The more discoverable your book is on Amazon, the more chances you will convert customers into buyers. It's one big vicious cycle.

How do you convert more customers into buyers? You got it – reviews! A product with five reviews is 270% more likely to sell than a product with no reviews.[1] Wow! Is that all it takes? Five reviews? Yep, even if you got your mom, her best friend, your cousin, significant other, and neighbor to leave a review. You're more likely to sell your book than your competitor, who has a big ol' fat goose egg for reviews. Of course, I'm not encouraging you to get your friends and family to leave a review. We'll address why that's not a good idea later in this book.

Other areas to consider the efficacy of having reviews is through advertising campaigns. Whether you're driving traffic natively through Amazon Advertising or delivering traffic through Facebook Ads, having your book equipped with some reviews is better than no reviews at all. There's a good reason Amazon loads up every product page with similar books and other products customers might enjoy. If your book doesn't convert a sale, Amazon still has a little more skin in the game. If you don't profit or capitalize on the traffic, then Amazon will.

Do you want to have a better return on your investment in paid advertising campaigns? Then, load your book up with reviews before you launch your next campaign. Once the traffic arrives at your book's product page, they at least have some proof other customers have read or bought your book before.

In *Amazon Keywords for Books*, I discussed the importance of relevancy. The Amazon algorithm places value on your product based on its ability to sell to customers at any given moment – also known as relevancy. The more relevant your book is, the more apt Amazon is to serve it to customers searching for it. What is the best builder in relevance for a product on Amazon? You guessed it – sales!

The more sales you get, the more relevant your title is in its given niche. What we know about relevance is that the algorithm doesn't simply rely on sales alone. Otherwise, brand new products with little to no sales would not appear in search queries. Sharing a product through social media, saving a product to wish lists, and getting reviews also play a role in building relevance.

Amazon views action taken on any given product page as a small trigger. This engagement sends a signal to the Amazon algorithm that says, "There's something about this product that other people might like."

That's where reviews come in. Every time a customer leaves a review, that sends a small signal to the Amazon algorithm. Furthermore, any keywords or commentary relative to your niche mentioned in the review also send signals to the Amazon algorithm. If someone votes for a review as helpful or comments on a review, additional signals are sent to the algorithm.

What goes up inevitably comes down. Getting reviews and engagement on a page may be effective in the moment, but it doesn't have lasting power in building relevance. That's not to say the social proof isn't as compelling on the browsing customer. Those reviews will still hold weight with the browsing customer. Similar to a balloon tossed in the air, the relevancy slowly drifts down for a product. The further out we go from a posted review, the less it affects the product's relevance.

Don't let that stop you. Should you accept it, your mission is to continue to bring in a consistent flow of reviews. That way, you prove to the Amazon algorithm how relevant your title truly is compared to other titles or books with less or older reviews. The key to building long-term sustainable relevancy in the Amazon algorithm is getting more sales. If you want more sales, then get more reviews.

Legendary guitarist, Dimebag Darrell, was once told by his father if he learned one riff a day over the year, he'd have learned 365 new riffs. Similar to Darrell, if you focus on getting one new review every day, you'll have 365 reviews in a year. If that seems impossible, then consider getting one review per week – fifty-two reviews in a year. Consistency is the name of the game. Stick to gathering reviews, and you'll have a ton of reviews to build massive social proof. Meanwhile, you'll keep the relevancy balloon afloat by tapping it up and away from the floor.

Keeping your product relevant will deliver more traffic. In turn, you should see more opportunities to sell more books. One hand washes the other, and you hopefully get more reviews.

Is it a good idea to get reviews all at once, or does it work against you? It's certainly debatable how a large influx of reviews will hurt your book. However, it does prove to Amazon the title might not have good long-term sustainability. Sure, it's great to see a title sell many books on launch day, and it's even nicer to have scores of reviews shower in after launch. What's even better is a gradual influx of reviews. Stick with it and never give up on the mission to bring in more reviews.

What about bad reviews? Do low-star reviews bring down your book? There are a couple of ways to look at this issue. If you have nothing but four and five-star reviews, browsing customers might feel suspicious. After all, we're in the day and age where fake reviews run afoul of Amazon on the regular. Having a few low reviews helps balance out a product page. Book reviews seem more authentic when there are all types of customers' experiences and mindsets shared in a review.

Where one customer might dislike a certain aspect of a book, another might find it appealing. For instance, one customer might leave a low rating and state:

"This book was too detailed and spent way too much time describing the scene. Cut to the chase, I just want the fight scene."

Another customer might read that low review and think:

"Well, that's just my style of reading. I hate it when writers rush into a fight scene. I like it when a writer develops the character, lays out the scene, and builds suspense to a dramatic climax."

One man's trash is another man's treasure. We often assume this phrase is only applicable to physical objects. In this instance, one person's dislike could strike the other person's fancy.

While a low review doesn't give the greatest feeling, it can serve the bigger picture. Take it with a grain of salt and remind yourself, you cannot please everyone. Once you get good with that fact, receiving the bad news of a low review becomes easier.

Good, bad, or indifferent; reviews play a large role in developing trust with your potential customer. How many you get is not as relevant as how many you get consistently over the long term. I heard a famous YouTuber state how no book will have any long-lasting power unless it had fifty reviews.

Fifty reviews, huh? This same famous YouTuber isn't prolific. She has a handful of publications. Where she gets her information is unknown. You can't discern that fifty reviews answer the long-term success when you haven't at least published hundreds of books to be statistically relevant. Ultimately, there's no hard and fast number of reviews to determine your book's long-term success. Even the previous stats I shared about five reviews versus none is somewhat anecdotal since results can vary based on the product type, the niche, and the buying audience.

Buyers like to see reviews on a product. Some reviews are better than no reviews. Never has a customer landed on a product, found the number of reviews to be below fifty, and clicked away. It's just not a thing. There's no real hard evidence the Amazon algorithm will favor a product because it has fifty reviews. What does the algorithm favor? Consistent performance. So long as the product continues to sell and get consistent reviews, the Amazon algorithm rewards that product.

Though fifty reviews are an admirable goal, once you hit the milestone, go for an even higher goal. As you're shooting for your goals, remember it will take time and consistent efforts. Along the way, you will get organic reviews. However, you shouldn't rely solely on organic reviews to keep your book relevant to Amazon.

I often hear it takes 1000 ebook downloads before you get one organic review. Wow! If that were true, it'd take you 50,000 downloads to even hit a fifty-review milestone. If you're getting 50,000 downloads or purchases, then chances are pretty likely you're getting more than organic reviews along the way. On most occasions, authors aren't even getting 50,000 downloads with a deep back catalog of books. It's sad but true.

I implore you not to be complacent. Do not rely on organic reviews and consider them more like icing on the cake. They're nice to have, but you shouldn't rely on them to happen. If you were to bank on organic reviews, your strategy needs to change from gathering reviews to selling more books. While I encourage you to pump up your book sales through marketing and promotion, you shouldn't let review gathering fall to the wayside.

Reviews ▼ **Adhering to Amazon Community Guidelines** 🔍

I have to open this chapter with the compulsory disclaimer: Amazon didn't endorse, fund, or agree to this book. They can and will change their community guidelines. Rather than creating a brand-new edition for every change Amazon makes in their rules, I'm just going to defer you to them first. Sadly, no book will be evergreen with the ever-changing market online. Still, I'm going to do my best to give you the currently acceptable practices and recommendations according to the current Amazon Community Guidelines.

First and foremost, customers cannot post a product review without spending $50 over the past year. If you send people to leave a review, they need to spend the minimum first.[2]

A few years ago, Amazon caught wind of some bad actors posting fake reviews on product pages. It mostly involved third-party sellers and some self-publishers. These bad actors would hire outside parties to post reviews on their product page to bolster relevancy in the search engine. They tricked Amazon customers into believing their product had real reviews.

Rather than kick everyone out for posting bad reviews, Amazon placed a paywall to deter bad actors. It still hasn't entirely stopped all bad actors; it's simply slowed them down. After all, where there's a will, there's a way. Bad actors will hire outside parties plus give a $50 allowance to spend on Amazon. They can then use it to buy a ton of books, inflate the book rank, and then leave reviews wherever they want.

Here's the interesting part: anyone can leave any review on any product they wish, so long as they fulfill the $50 minimum spending threshold. That means customers don't even have to buy a specific product on Amazon to leave a review. For instance, if a customer bought your book at the local bookstore and met the Amazon minimum spending threshold, he can post a review on your book on Amazon.

However, Amazon labels the review differently based on the person's purchase history on the website. When a customer buys a product on Amazon and leaves a review, Amazon labels the review as a "Verified Purchase."

Whereas, if a customer didn't buy a product on Amazon but leaves a product review, Amazon doesn't label it. Most industry insiders refer to this type of review as an "Unverified Purchase." Anyone can leave a review on any product on Amazon. As long as a customer purchases $50 in Amazon products in the last year, he can post a review of anything.

What has more traction, the verified purchase, or unverified purchase? Amazon never states if the verified purchase tag carries any more weight than the unverified purchase review.[3] While some industry experts feel it does carry more weight in the algorithm, there's no solid proof. If we consider the customers, do they really care about the *Verified Purchase* tag? I can guarantee you most customers aren't even aware of it.

In fact, in the launch of *Amazon Keywords for Books,* quite a few readers who received an advanced reading copy weren't aware of the $50 threshold. Chances are likely they didn't even know about verified purchase reviews too. The tag isn't too conspicuous on the reviews. In some instances, it's so small on a desktop computer most people won't even notice it.

The "Verified Purchase" review tag displays a
proof of purchase for the reviewer.

The day might come when Amazon has enough of the bad actors and unverified purchase reviews. Then, they will require customers to buy the product to leave a review. If a customer doesn't buy the product through Amazon, then his opinion isn't welcome. I imagine those old unverified purchase reviews would disappear, and all that would remain are the verified purchase reviews.

If you want to be on the safe side, try to get verified purchase reviews when you can. Sure, it's easier said than done, but it could very well help you out. Even if Amazon never removes the ability to post unverified purchase reviews, at least you have some verified purchase reviews for more credibility.

Biased Reviews Could Kill Your Momentum

Back when I first self-published, I naturally wanted to post a review of my product. Taking a little extra time, I crafted the perfect review of my first book. Once I posted the review, I was sure it'd create more intrigue and draw prospective buyers. I waited a day or two to see if it'd post on my book's product page, and nothing surfaced.

Realizing it might seem kind of sad to review my own book, I reached out to my wife to post a review. She, too, wrote up a brilliant review and posted it. This time the review stuck, but within a few days, the review disappeared. Undeterred, she tried again with the same results.

Naturally, I contacted Amazon support only to find out one glaring issue. If Amazon detects a direct relationship between a product and a buyer, they determine the review as biased. While posting a review of my own book is rather sad, it's also very biased. Amazon does not want biased reviews. The relationship between a seller and a customer influences the review. Amazon doesn't want any of that bias. After all, the customer isn't going to remain impartial.

Your mother, brother, sister, wife, close friends, or anyone who's currently living with you will stand to gain something out of leaving a positive review. That just won't work. Amazon simply wants candid thoughts from customers who don't stand to gain anything out of leaving a review. As a customer, I'm sure you would agree too. You don't want to buy a product when all you see are positive marks posted by the seller's mother. Any customer wants real insights and reflections so he can make an informed purchase without coercion or shenanigans.

What constitutes a biased review beyond people you directly know? Well, the guidelines get a bit gray, and the automated systems indicate a double standard. Amazon has what appears to be an automated system vetting reviews posted on its platform. If a seller and buyer share the same Amazon account, physical address, bank account, or credit card, Amazon deems the review biased. Instantly, the review is null and void.

Amazon also flags reviews as biased for what the reviewer states. If a reviewer posts a specific word or phrase indicating a direct relationship, they'll pull it. The company isn't fully disclosing what those words or phrases are. It makes sense for Amazon to keep those words and phrases undisclosed, so bad actors don't have the opportunity to work their way around the system.

We could assume any word or phrase indicating a direct relationship would be off the table. If a reviewer states he's your best friend and loves your book, don't be surprised when Amazon pulls the review down. If you have a reader who posted a review, it's going to be up to that reader to address the removed review, not you. It only further complicates the situation and proves a direct relationship when you get involved.

Ultimately, we're subject to the whim of a machine that detects bias, and we have no control over what it deems as biased or not. Rather than sweat the system, keep pushing forward and gathering reviews that will stick. You can always direct your reader to address the issue with Amazon at community-help@amazon.com.

Friends & Family Are Killing Your Book

New authors should bask in the admiration of their peers, friends, and family when they first publish a book. It's quite the feat and not something too many people can or will do. I won't take anything away from the power of having a great support network. When you publish your first book, everyone and your mother will want a copy for prosperity's sake.

Sadly, your friends and family are killing the relevancy of your book. We already know getting a review from your family is a no-go. If Amazon detects a direct relationship, the review will never see the light of day.

For the sake of argument, let's say your friends and family have no issue leaving a review, and the review sticks with no further complication. That's all well and good, except now, you confused the Amazon algorithm. Previously covered in *Amazon Keywords for Books*, the algorithm is a machine-generated formula tracking buyer behaviors and predicting outcomes on the platform. The algorithm is largely responsible for predicting and serving up products customers will most likely want to buy.

No, you didn't confuse the Amazon algorithm with undetected, yet biased reviews. You confused the algorithm when you allowed your friends and family to buy your book. Though your friends and family love you and have your back, they may not necessarily enjoy the type of content you write. Rarely do your writing interests overlap with your family or friends' reading interests. Therein lies the problem.

When you have a friend or family member support you when buying and reviewing your book, you're having them confuse the algorithm. Where the Amazon algorithm expects specific buy patterns based on your family and friends' buy history, a curveball comes out of nowhere.

For example, suppose your mother normally buys books based on gardening and products for her garden. In that case, the Amazon algorithm serves products to her based on her interests in gardening. Once your mom buys your book based on adult baby diaper lover (ABDL) romance, she confuses the algorithm. The Amazon machine needs to figure out the sudden shift in buying and reviewing patterns, and then it tries to match up your ABDL romance book with other gardeners. You can imagine most gardeners will give that ABDL romance book a hard pass, thereby decreasing relevancy in the search engine.

Avoid selling your books to friends and family and having them leave a review. If they must buy your book, then let them do it. I wouldn't recommend pushing them to leave a review. Just leave it alone and go on without it.

The Bias in Social Media

Now more than ever, building an author platform requires having a presence on social media. As an author, you can create a stronger bond with your readers, develop a sense of community, and grow your author brand quicker than ever.

Lurking in Facebook Groups, online forums, and chats is a bit of an enigma – bias through social media. Some authors believe Amazon tracks all online social media activity. The theory is if an author and reader connect in any way via social media, Amazon strikes down any review posted.

This theory means if you and your reader are friends on Facebook, then Amazon deems this a direct relationship. Therefore, any review posted by your reader has a bias. In 2015, a reader had some issues with review removal. This reader followed her favorite author on social media. That was the only direct connection she could draw to why the review disappeared.[4]

Some people even speculate if a reader likes an author's business page, Amazon views it as a direct relationship. It's no surprise how it's harder than ever to separate fact from fiction. Meanwhile, Amazon isn't being entirely transparent about its methods for determining bias in reviews. When pressed for an answer, Amazon simply states a detection of a direct relationship.

How is Amazon able to police such a large area, and is it legal? These are certainly questions worth considering for another book altogether. For now, let's focus on what we can do to mitigate any issues. It all starts with the direct correlation between Amazon and social media.

For starters, Amazon bought the social media platform for readers called Goodreads in 2013. One of the ways users can log into Goodreads is through a Facebook login. This integration opens up more questions about how Amazon and Facebook could be data mining together in a collaborative effort. During this data mining, can Amazon see who associates with whom on the Facebook platform?

Dave Chesson, of the YouTube channel Kindlepreneur,[5] even questioned this potential correlation between Goodreads and Facebook. When a review disappears, and the only trackable evidence comes down to this relationship between social media platforms, it makes you wonder. When setting up a Goodreads account, Dave recommends you avoid signing in with Facebook, and use an altogether different login.

This safeguard is something you can always share with your readers. Still, it's certainly not something you should make part of your review gathering methods. I simply want to shed light on potential reasons reviews might disappear from your book's product page.

Review Swaps Are the Worst

In the early days of publishing on Amazon, authors could get more reviews through a quid pro quo system called review swapping. One author could exchange books with another author. They'd each read the book and then leave an honest review on the product page. Both authors walked away happy, and life was good.

Sadly, what was once a good idea, turned into a bad idea quickly. Bad actors rolled in and bastardized the system. Rather than exchanging with other authors, the bad actors hired outside workers to do their dirty work. Instead of reading the book, the hired help (aka virtual assistants) reached out to other authors or people in their field. They do the exchange and post a review despite never having read the book.

In some instances, the book reviews often appear stilted and are pretty bland like, "This is a good book. I would recommend it to you. You should buy this book. You would like it too."

Author review swaps are in direct violation of the Amazon Community Guidelines. You must not coerce or pay for reviews. If you do either of those, you stand to lose a lot. In fact, I know first-hand the consequences.

In 2014, everyone and their mother published books on the Kindle Direct Publishing (KDP) platform. Anyone could publish just about any level of hammered garbage and profit hand over fist. Naturally, overnight success stories and would-be experts cropped up, seemingly popping out of the woodwork. The name of the game was to make as much money as you could regardless of the rules Amazon laid out. Part of the bad advice was to get reviews through author review swaps.

Naively, I bought in despite knowing author review swaps were, at the very least, garnering biased reviews for my titles. Having to connect with authors and getting to know them personally would imply I had a direct relationship. Yet, I soldiered forward confident I wasn't hurting anyone. The more reviews I racked up for my title, the more my books sold and climbed the charts. It seemed like the fun would never end until it did.

Around June 2015, word spread about Amazon clamping down on fake reviews and author review swaps. By this time, I was running on all cylinders. I easily read dozens of books and painstakingly crafted beautiful reviews for the authors. I even scaled it up to a point where I hired a virtual assistant to alleviate the workload. Hiring out would be my undoing.

One day, I checked into one of my books to verify a posted review from an author swap. Not only was the review gone, but scores of reviews vanished. Primarily, the bad and poorly written reviews were the ones to disappear. My heart sank, and a feeling of defeat set in.

"That's okay," I thought, "at least I still have my reviews."

Fat chance! I opened my Amazon Reviewer profile to discover all my reviews weren't there. Every last review I posted since using Amazon – from books to supplements to movies – was history. I knew I was in trouble. After repeated attempts to contact Amazon over a few days, I finally received a response.

Amazon called me out for manipulating the reviews system and permanently banned me from using any of the Amazon Community features. As you can imagine, I lost reviewing privileges, commenting privileges, and the ability to partake in any future programs of the Amazon Community.

All this had to do was over my impatience to get reviews the legitimate way. Folks do not, under any circumstances, pay for an Amazon review or post a fake review. They will catch you, and they will enforce their community guidelines. To this day, I nervously look over my shoulder, wondering if this misdeed will create an issue with my other Amazon accounts. Could it affect all my Amazon accounts, including KDP, Merch by Amazon, Amazon Associates, Prime Video Direct, Media on Demand, and Twitch? Only time will tell.

If you're going to get reviews, do it without an exchange of money or through coercive practices like review swapping. It'll land you in hot water. Though my story seems pretty serious, it pales in comparison to the controversy surrounding a famous indie author, Chance Carter.

Bribes for Reviews

Around mid-2018, Amazon rolled out changes based on incentivizing reviews. What were the grounds for this sudden change? Authors were actively soliciting their readers for reviews. On the surface, asking your readers for reviews seems okay. That is until you bribe them. Romance author Chance Carter openly solicited his readers with the prospect of winning *Tiffany's Jewelry*. With proof of a posted review, Carter entered his readers in a giveaway for free jewelry. Enticing readers with the prospect of winning jewelry clearly creates biased reviews. In turn, the reviews will come out in favor of the book and the author.[6]

When Amazon caught wind of this indiscretion, they closed up the loophole. Chance Carter faced updating a deep backlist of titles. The lesson is, don't try to bribe or coerce your readers into leaving a review. You will get burned and have fewer reviews than when you started. Besides, do you really want to blow your marketing budget on jewelry for your readers? I think that's a bit overboard for reviews alone.

Without incentivizing or having any direct relationship with the reader, how can you get book reviews then? Surely, it can't be as hard as some people make it out to be, is it? Let's dive into the best first steps in getting reviews – inside the book.

When getting reviews, start with the path of least resistance. Meet your readers precisely where they're at – inside the book. Where you place it and how you ask are the most important aspects of getting reviews. Just remember, you don't want to deviate too far off the beaten path or go south of Amazon's Community Guidelines.

The best way to get reviews is simply to ask. That's it! Nothing fancy. The answer is always "no" if you never ask, and this area is no exception to the rule. Your approach is going to make the most difference. Simply asking alone won't get many results. Then again, if you go too long in your ask, you might get a lot of readers tuning out, especially where I'm going to have you insert it.

All ebooks on Amazon finish with a call-to-action (CTA) by Amazon to post a review. Even if you didn't follow my instructions, you could feel confident you have safety measures in place. Also, Amazon has readers sign into their associated Goodreads accounts. Then, readers can post on Amazon and Goodreads.

However, the reality is most readers won't finish your book. For that matter, some readers will most likely finish the last chapter and whatever comes after is inessential. The back matter of the book is what readers often overlook. The inessential content to them includes the author's bio, the special thanks, the resources, and the additional promotion of your other books.

If a reader is most likely to tune out after flipping the final page, we need to strike while the iron is hot! As soon as your book finishes, you need to lead with a CTA. Ask them for the review immediately after the last chapter. You only have one opportunity, so make the most of it.

Lead with a bold headline that commands their attention. Think about making the headline no more than five to six words long. If you're good at copywriting, then now is your time to shine! If you're like me and don't have the skillset, that's okay. Try your best.

The next thing is to keep it short. I recently checked out an indie author's book and discovered their CTA for leaving a review was over a page and a half long. No! I'm not reading your CTA. After all, I just finished your book, so what makes you think I'm going to read something that has no real intrinsic value for me? You need to lead with the goods.

Keep it simple. For instance:

> Now that you finished reading this book, it'd be a huge favor to me, and future readers, if you left feedback on Amazon.
>
> While I have no expectations on what kind of review you leave, it'd certainly make my day knowing you read the whole book and shared your honest experience with the world.
>
> You can post a review on Amazon or at Amazon.com/gp/product-review/B08HMCNKVT.

Feel free to swipe the copy above if you want, but I recommend rewording and rewriting it in a way to make sense for your book and brand.

Again, I'm not a copywriter, so you may want to consider dressing yours up in a more enticing way. The keys to a good CTA for reviewing include:

- Bold headline

- Brevity

- Outbound link

The last key to getting the review is to remove any hurdles for your reader. Instead of having your reader search for where to leave a review, send them right to the source. Sure, you could tell them to flip all the way to the back until Amazon asks them to leave a review. Might I suggest having them do less, though? Simply use an outbound link, and it's quite simple. The formula for the review website URL is:

Amazon.com/gp/product-review/(Insert your book ASIN here)

Let's first address the ASIN or American Standard Identification Number. The ASIN is the code associated with your book once you publish it to the Amazon platform. You can access it in your Kindle Direct Publishing dashboard next to your book or on your book's product page in the "Product Details" section. You will not have the ASIN until you publish the book.

Here's where I'm going to save you a lot of time and heartache. In *Promotional Strategies for Books*, I shared the importance of getting your own website and custom domain name. Furthermore, I suggested installing Pretty Links, a WordPress plug-in, so you could create subdirectories (i.e., dalelinks.com/checklist). Now, we're going to put your domain name to work.

Instead of having to update your publications when they launch with an unmemorable hyperlink, you're going to use a custom URL to redirect readers to the review page. For example, in *Amazon Keywords for Books*, my CTA for reviews included the link DaleLinks. com/ReviewKeywordsBook. Though the link wasn't working when I uploaded the ebook and print book, I had it working as soon as I knew the ASIN of my book.

You'll take the long Amazon link, add your ASIN to the end, and use your custom domain to redirect to the review page. You're done! This link will work for reviewing both your ebook and print book. If you don't fix the link right away, it's not a big deal. You won't have to sweat anyone using the review link right away since it's at the end of the book. And, no one will skip to the end once they buy it in the first twenty-four hours anyway.

Just make sure you don't forget to create the custom domain redirect as soon as your book is live on Amazon. That way, you aren't panicking later when you realize the custom domain isn't set.

The nice thing is you'll have a web address you can recommend your readers visit. Share it in your email newsletter, on social media, or in a video interview. The options are limitless.

The smartest thing to do is use a custom domain name with brand recognition and make the subdirectory easily memorable. Don't put a ton of initials, numbers, or acronyms. You want people to remember it or trust it when they see it.

While posting a CTA in the back of your book might seem rather innocuous, it's much better than trying to go without it. Also, I find it mind-blowing how authors don't have this simple feature in their books. Inserting a CTA in a book seems like a given to most indie authors. Yet, quite a few authors who struggle to get reviews aren't even doing it. Don't be that guy. Insert a CTA in the back of your book. You'll thank me later.

*N*ow that you have a fundamental understanding of reviews, and how to get them, it's time to break outside your inner circle and reach out into the world. Where do you look, who can you trust, and what should you say?

The first place to look is through a simple Google search. Type in your niche and book reviews. Skip the ads. We're only interested in a specific type of book reviewer. Some readers loyally follow and support their favorite niche. On their websites or blogs, they share candid reviews of what they've read. On many occasions, they don't cost a dime, and quite frankly, they shouldn't. Remember, we don't want to pay for reviews posted on Amazon.

Next, dig through the blogger's website to verify the type of reviews they do. Some of them only post reviews to their websites while others post on Amazon as well. It's not a deal-breaker for me if they don't post to Amazon. I'm less apt to send the first review copies to readers who aren't actively posting on Amazon. I may come back to them later once I have courted all the active Amazon reviewers.

Do a little research ahead, and it will pay off in the long run. If a blogger has an Amazon reviewer profile, read through their old reviews. You're looking for a historical pattern. Some reviewers are fairly balanced and will leave a mix of good and bad reviews. Then, other reviewers might leave a ton of low reviews or nothing but high reviews. I tend to avoid anyone with a profile with historically low reviews. This reader tends to be fickle and not worth approaching. If you see an average of four to five-star reviews, then this reader might be a good fit!

Now, search for any contact information and guidelines. You can find most of this info on the main landing page or the about page of the website. It might take a minute or two but can be worth it. Once you have the info you need, reach out to them. I'll explain how you pitch it once you consider other avenues to contact reviewers.

We're in a new age where video is king online! If you can land a review with a video creator, you've greatly increased your odds of getting more sales. YouTube, Facebook Live, Twitch, Periscope, and any other video platform are places to start. You'll search just as you did on Google. This time pay the closest attention to video creators with a history of posting book reviews.

YouTube has a growing community of video creators aptly named BookTubers (or BookTube). Their main focus is on books. They read books, share books they buy, and interact with other readers. Think of it as a Book Club, but on video. Again, focus on BookTubers actively posting reviews on Amazon and are familiar with your niche. You don't want to send a review copy of your werebear shapeshifter romance book if the BookTuber primarily talks about science fiction fantasy books.

The next best people to contact are podcasters. Downloadable audio has been an upward trend, and it seems almost everyone has a podcast about something these days. Do the same simple Google search you did for book review sites, but this time look for podcasts instead of book reviewers. If you happen to find a podcaster who does reviews, then great! In most instances, you just want to find a podcast relevant to your niche. Then, it's up to you to do the outreach.

Asking for a Review from a Complete Stranger

Do you remember the call-to-action we placed in the back of your book? We're going to use the same methodology in asking for a review. You won't need a special link. In fact, you won't even need to send any content when you're cold prospecting.

The key to outreach is brevity. You must respect the potential readers' time. Imagine how easy it is to find them. Now think about how many other authors are contacting them for reviews. Respect their time, and it may pay off in dividends.

When it comes to what you say, I recommend you speak from the heart. You don't need to go into too much detail. If you've done your research, you can probably lead with how you found the reviewer and what you like best about their content. The next step is to skip right to the chase. Why are you contacting them, and what's in it for them?

Don't beat around the bush. You're looking for readers who'd be willing to read a complimentary copy in hopes of getting honest reviews posted on Amazon. That's it! Don't worry about Jedi mind tricks or writing the best ad copy to entice them to accept your offer.

Here's an example:

Hey, Dale,

Your YouTube channel popped up while I was kicking around online, and I noticed you're a big fan of werebear shapeshifter romance.

I'd love to get your feedback on my upcoming release called "werebear versus werewolf."

If you're game, I could send you a copy right away.

Thanks for your time, and I'm looking forward to hearing back from you.

Did you notice how brief I kept it? It didn't take much time to type it. Simultaneously, the recipient won't feel overwhelmed by an epic-length email that doesn't get to the point. Cut to the chase, and you'll waste less of everyone's time.

Do not send a copy to your prospect without getting permission. I know it seems easy to attach your ebook to an email. Still, nothing seems fishier than an email from a random stranger with an attachment. Whenever I get an email with an attachment from a stranger, I toss it into my spam folder.

Also, some reviewers have a format preference. You'll want to have your ebook available in PDF, epub, and mobi, so it's readable across all devices. I typically upload all three formats into a zipped file with instructions on downloading the preferred file to mobile. Then, I put the zipped file into a cloud drive and generate a shareable link for the potential reviewer.

Another reason to avoid sending out a manuscript without permission is some reviewers prefer hard copies of your book. Quite frankly, a vast majority of readers still prefer print books. The part you need to consider is, can you afford to send out print copies? You'll have to account for all the costs. Sending out a review copy through Amazon is one way and probably the cheapest solution if you have Amazon Prime. Another way is to order bulk copies and then send out the review copy. The latter method requires a bit more money and hassle.

The issue with gifting a copy to a reviewer from your own account is that Amazon might deem the review biased. Because of the connection between you and the reader through your Amazon purchase, Amazon can then assume you know this person directly. Sadly, the more costly and difficult option of ordering copies in advance might be the better option for review longevity.

It's not to say you can't gift print copies or ebooks to a reviewer. I've done it many times with no issue with the reviews sticking. Consider two factors in the efficacy of that review:

- The reader will post a review from their account, so the review will be an unverified purchase

- If the reader has the same address on file for their Amazon account as the one you shipped to, Amazon might deem it as biased

There's no real way of telling how Amazon enforces it. If you want to err on the side of caution, simply fulfill the print shipment yourself.

Some time ago, I gathered reviews for my book *An Ultimate Home Workout Plan Bundle*. For whatever reason, I felt sending print copies to every reviewer was a great idea. I reached out to several reviewers on Amazon, a few bloggers, and various influencers. All in all, I invested over $300 in about thirty-six review copies. These three mistakes were the result:

1. Investing in print copies when I couldn't even afford the expense.

2. Neglecting the ebook option.

3. I didn't account for the review copy ratio. You'll learn more about that next.

Gathering Reviews: The Numbers Game

In most instances, getting reviews is a numbers game. The more people you ask, the better. I found one out of every three readers will post a review after receiving a complimentary copy. This includes following up with readers. Some readers will be on top of posting their reviews. Most readers will spend their time doing other things outside of reading the book. A fraction of readers will simply become unresponsive. Yes, it's the harsh truth, you can send out free stuff to someone, and they'll stop talking to you.

Indie author Alinka Rutkowska shared in a post on Kindlepreneur.com about her experience in getting reviews. She discussed how getting reviews is a numbers game. Only one in three readers will post a review even when the agreement was to post a review for getting a complimentary copy. If you want 300 reviews, then you're going to need to get 900 readers for your book.[7]

Do not make the same mistakes I did. Never invest money into review gathering you can't stand to lose. Offer the ebook before suggesting the print book is available. Sending out ebooks is way more cost-effective and less time-consuming than print books. Lastly, never expect to get all readers to post a review. I never heard of any author having a 100% return on their review efforts. If a reader doesn't post a review, put them on a *Do Not Contact* list and move on.

When you find a reviewer who posts a review and doesn't need prompting, hang onto them. Cherish that reader and show your appreciation. No, you don't have to shower them with jewelry. A simple thanks via email will suffice, or even classier, a short video. If the person is an influencer, YouTuber, or blogger, it behooves you to showcase their review and promote their brand. That's the best gratitude you can give to influencers.

The Follow-Up Sequence

One area to further consider is your follow-up sequence. You need to build reasonable time to follow up after the reader receives your review copy. Ask the reader when a good time is to follow up with them. Don't overthink it. The reader is attending to other things outside of reading your book. If you have a standard-length book between 20,000 and 40,000 words, then a month should be sufficient. A reader will need considerably more time with an epic-length novel. The best way to know how long it'll take a reader is to ask them. That's it!

When I follow up, I do it once and move on. I won't bother with hounding readers about leaving reviews. I'd rather spend time writing my next book, gathering more reviews, or promoting my other books. Trying to micromanage readers is time-consuming and, quite frankly, comes off as desperate. It's not a good look, so follow up once, then move on.

Chasing after influencers, bloggers, and YouTubers can be tiring. Part of why it sucks comes from the act of cold prospecting. If you're anything like me, then you most likely despise being salesy or coming off as pushy. That predisposition tends to make most people avoid cold prospecting altogether. It's not that cold prospecting is bad. It's just hard work. You'll get more no's than yes's. Even when they accept you, you'll face the harsh reality that only one in three readers leaves a review.

That's okay because I have your solution - an advanced reader copy team! Also known as an ARC team, the advanced reader copy team is an elite group of readers who receive your manuscript before the public. The ARC team functions in two ways:

- Early feedback

- Immediate reviews after publishing

Getting early feedback from readers can help you fine-tune any small discrepancies. For instance, when I launched *Amazon Keywords for Books,* I reached out to about twelve followers. I had these twelve readers opt into the ARC team by way of StoryOrigin. They had the option to download any ebook format – epub, mobi, or PDF. Within the first twenty-four hours, I found a litany of issues with the manuscript. Between formatting errors, missing text, and typos, I snuffed out those issues well before it hit the buying public.

I guess you could say your ARC team functions as a last line of defense in proofreading before the book goes public. Be mindful of what your ARC readers say and the problems they point out. Don't get defensive. After all, they're helping you free of charge. If you don't understand the criticism, have the reader clarify. It's better to know than to assume.

The second most important function of an ARC team is getting reviews out on launch day. These reviews are critical in lending credibility as soon as your book goes live on the Amazon Marketplace. Once browsing customers land on your product page, they'll see immediately other people read your book. That warm, fuzzy feeling of knowing another reader consumed your book is more validation working in your favor.

How exactly do you build an ARC team? What if you don't have a following? Is this even possible for all authors? It requires a deeper explanation. In short, ARC teams should be part of any author's book launch strategy. Without one, you're taking a gamble and hoping Amazon will push your book based on keyword and niche selection alone.

Building an Email List

Email marketing is a vehicle all authors need to have in their marketing and promotion toolbox. By using services like Mailchimp, MailerLite, ConvertKit, and the like, you can solicit your readers to subscribe to your email newsletter. In *Promotional Strategies for Books*, I shared insights on the best ways to build and grow an email list.

In brief, email marketing is a safeguard for your business. Though people who read your books are your readers, they are not your customers.

They are Amazon's customers. It's the cold, hard truth. If Amazon should ever deem you unfit to be on their platform, they can and will kick you off the platform without any recourse. Rather than tempt fate, you should put a system in place that converts your readers into your followers. How do you do that? Email marketing!

Now it doesn't require a ton of coding or technical know-how. All you need to do is join any number of email marketing services available. Then, create a simple opt-in page through the platform. Once you complete the landing page, your email marketing platform will give you a URL or web address. Share that link with your readers.

Start with inserting a call-to-action (CTA) in the front and back of your book. Place a short prompt before your introduction. Having it in your book's front matter helps, especially since most people will not read an entire book. For my front matter CTA, I lead with something compelling and an offer the reader can't refuse. Try to entice them with a special offer for subscribing to your email newsletter. It could be something as simple as:

> Want to know the secret to publish less while profiting more?
>
> Then download a free copy to the Smart Publisher's Black Book when you subscribe to Dale's VIP Reader's Club.
>
> Visit DaleLinks.com/Checklist to join today!

Though it's a crude example, an offer like this one works, nonetheless. The main thing is to attract the type of email subscribers you want, so only offer what you can deliver and what interests them most. If you're dry on ideas on how to entice your readers, then try something like:

> Do you want to get updated news about publishing, discounts, and advanced copies?
>
> Then, join Dale's VIP Reader's Club at DaleLinks.com/SignUp.

Some email marketing experts would lose their minds over this simple CTA because you'll get fewer email subscribers. Don't worry about what they think. The best part of a simple CTA is you're going to get the cream of the crop--the super-fans. These are folks who don't need much reason to join your email newsletter. On most occasions, building a list on a simple CTA will be a more engaged list.

The primary goal of building an email list is so you can take your readers with you wherever you wish to go. It's your insurance policy against the worst. The next goal is to engage, interact, and deliver value with your email subscribers. It's not enough to get them to subscribe to your email newsletter. You must interact with them. How do you measure the effectiveness of your email marketing efforts? You need to get your subscribers opening the emails, clicking on your offers, and possibly buying what you have to offer.

Building an ARC Team with Your Email List

The best first step in building an ARC team with your email list is by asking for advanced readers in an email campaign. You don't need to do anything fancy. Just ask if anyone would be interested in getting advanced copies of your book. Don't sweat having to explain how it works. You don't need to muddy up the waters with the intricacies. Just get interested readers.

You can handle interested parties in one of two ways:

1. Have your subscribers reply to your email and segment their email from the main email list. Every email marketing platform has different ways to segment an email list, so visit their FAQ section to find out how to do it.

2. You can send them to an ARC management platform. We'll discuss those options in a bit.

Long before there were ARC management platforms, I relied on segmenting my email subscribers who wanted to participate in the ARC team. To make sure I kept them in the loop on special deals, I usually moved them to a separate list altogether.

Let's say you don't want to fuss with the tire kickers and freebie seekers. Then, you may want to segment your email audience right away. You can start by segmenting your audience down to subscribers who have opened your email the most in the past thirty to ninety days. That means they're at least interested in reading your content. If you want to identify the subscribers most invested in your content, then identify subscribers who click on the most outbound links. These subscribers have proven they want to read your email and trust you enough to click on a recommended outbound link.

With segmentation comes the harsh reality you won't reach as many subscribers, but you'll remove the less motivated subscribers and skip right to the most interested ones. Think of it as a way of rewarding your subscribers for being extra cool in supporting you.

Once you have your hyper-engaged subscribers, send out your offer to join the ARC team. Keep the offer simple and straight to the point. It's not enough for you to ask them to join. You'll need to tell them what they get. Share what the book is, the potential release date, and maybe a short blurb about it. Have them reply to your email or click on a specific link to send them to a sign-up page.

Once a subscriber opts in to your ARC team, set expectations. Explain to them how an advanced reader copy works. You have to clearly state you're giving an advanced copy, hoping they'll leave a review. Don't tell them you require positive reviews or that they post on an exact date. Amazon gets a little finicky when you coerce readers into leaving reviews. If you find a reader isn't posting a review as you want, simply remove them from the ARC team.

At some point, you want to track the reviews. I use a simple spread-sheet through Google Sheets to track each ARC team member's name and email address. Ask your ARC team member what their Amazon reviewer name is. Once they post a review, you can then track it without having them report back. The less the ARC team has to do beyond reading and posting a review, the better. Though I still suggest asking the reader report back to you once they left a review. It isn't a require-ment, but it certainly makes life easy in tracking each review.

Follow up with your ARC team once before your book launches to let them know about the impending launch. Then, notify your ARC team after you publish your book. Let them know it's time to post their reviews. Again, don't push them to leave any type of review. Just encourage them to leave a review and share their thoughts, whether positive or negative.

After your book launches and your team posts reviews, keep an eye on who follows through. Give your ARC team at least a week to post the reviews. After the week is up, you can send a final follow-up and showcase some of the best reviews so far. That will get anyone lagging to finally post a review. Once you've sent out the last follow-up, remove any non-performing ARC team members. You don't need to send a break-up email, and don't worry about telling them they're gone. They'll simply know you removed them when they see future books posted without getting early access.

Building an ARC Team Through Website Services

Years ago, the option for building an ARC team beyond your email list wasn't as accessible. Using a website devoted to building an ARC team is a no-brainer. You don't have to worry about micromanaging your ARC team. The website handles all the review tracking and emails. You can continue to do other things outside of ARC team management.

Between BookSprout, BookFunnel, Prolific Works, and one I'm actively using, StoryOrigin, you have plenty of options. The biggest issue is going to come down to what you need and what discretionary expense you have. Remember, your time is finite, so do you want to painstakingly track an ARC team or have someone else do it for you.

The last major publication and hard launch I did was in 2016. I was happy to find options when jumping back into the game to release *Amazon Keywords for Books*. I didn't have to rely entirely on my email list. Even though I had an email list, I didn't want the hassle of hosting the ebook files, distributing it, tracking reviews, and the rest.

Naturally, I reached out to my friend Evan Gow at StoryOrigin. At the time of this book, StoryOrigin remains in open beta with free access to all the features. Since I was new to the service, it required a little trial and error.

To find the best services for your needs, you need to consider these options:

- **File storage** — Will the platform host your ebook files? What are the file size limitations?

- **Email acquisition** — Will the platform collect ARC readers' emails, and can you get access to those emails?

- **Follow up** — Will the platform follow up with your ARC team when your book launches?

- **Review tracking** — Does the platform track reviews? What types of reviews does the platform track beyond Amazon?

I discovered a few problems right away when using StoryOrigin. For *Amazon Keywords for Books*, I had a rather large file size due to the high-resolution images. I had to get with my interior formatting team to create a compressed version of the files. In turn, I needed to disclose a slight deviation in the files with future ARC team members. I didn't want potential team members to think they were getting the full file size that the buying public would get.

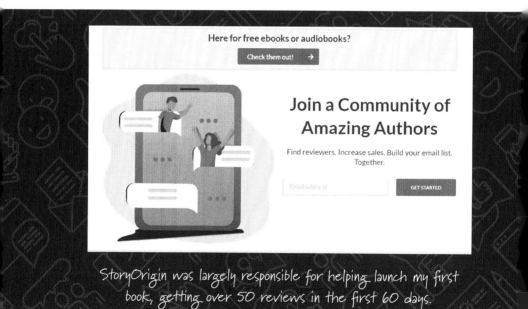

Here for free ebooks or audiobooks?

Check them out! →

Join a Community of Amazing Authors

Find reviewers. Increase sales. Build your email list. Together.

GET STARTED

StoryOrigin was largely responsible for helping launch my first book, getting over 50 reviews in the first 60 days.

The next issue I ran into was I didn't get the emails from each subscriber. Once the ARC team member posted a review, then I had access to them. At first, I was a bit sad, but when I reflected on it, I'd rather keep ARC members who have posted a review versus those who haven't. Sadly, I'll have to earmark the ARC members who didn't leave a review, so I reject them on future projects.

The final issue I have is the ARC team I built was only good for the current project. I couldn't simply carry the current ARC team over to the next project. Evan simply said I could reach out to those who left a review on the first project to join the new ARC team on the second project.

One of the nice parts about managing your ARC team yourself without a website service is moving the ARC team from one book project to the next without much fall off. This isn't a deal-breaker and will separate the wheat from the chaff. That's why I chose to stay with StoryOrigin. Oh, and it's free right now. I mean, come on! It's free! Can you blame me?

As for the other services, I hear a lot of good things about BookSprout. They run their services based on a tier system. You can get up to fifty reviews for about $10 per month. That's nice if you want to figure out the cost based on the review ratio shared earlier. If one in every three readers leave a review, then you can build an ARC team of up to 150 members and pay about $10 per month. Should you get more than fifty reviews, you pay $20 per month and the privilege of unlimited reviews.

If you're brand new to self-publishing and review gathering, I recommend sticking to what you can afford. While it's nice to have all the extra features in a premium service, you need to be realistic with where you are as an author. If free options are all you can afford, look into StoryOrigin or other no-cost alternatives.

*A*re paid reviews okay for your book on Amazon? According to Amazon Community Guidelines, you should not pay for any reviews posted on Amazon. While this rule is abundantly clear, many websites and services confuse authors with their contradictory information.

Why aren't paid reviews okay with Amazon? The online marketplace believes receiving payment in exchange for a review opens the door to many bad actors. If it's as simple as paying for a review, couldn't the person with the most money rise to the top of the charts?

Amazon wants a level playing field for all authors and sellers on their marketplace. Getting paid reviews is a no-go because many people would abuse this power and post fake reviews. However, some sites will have you believe otherwise. Let's address each type of paid service and sift through the good and the bad.

Paid Review Sites & Services

These types of services are cut and dry. You'll typically know who runs a good or bad service based on their claims. If a website promises a certain amount of reviews, then it's probably not a legitimate service. As you already learned, getting reviews is a numbers game. Though we can expect one out of every three readers to leave a review, it's not always guaranteed. Humans are imperfect, life gets in the way, and some readers will fall through.

When a website or service promises to deliver a set number of reviews, they have something happening behind the scenes. I spoke with one such service provider. His services offered guaranteed reviews and even had a guaranteed bestsellers service package. When asked how he could guarantee a set number of reviews, he shared that in-house staff would cover any missing reviews. Essentially, it came down to paying for a review if you aren't soliciting to a group of readers.

When you pay a reader to read your book, there will be a certain level of bias. There is an exception to paid reviews we'll discuss. For now, any time a service provider promises an exact number of readers and reviews, I'm always leery and cautious about using them.

Never, under any circumstances, hire a freelancer to review your book. Again, this comes down to a clear violation of Amazon guidelines. At least with the former option, you have some separation between you, the service provider, and the potential readers. With freelance websites, you actively violate the Amazon Guidelines. Should you get caught, you'll face the same consequences I did.

Then you have virtual assistant services that specialize in getting reviews. This area gets a bit dicey, and if you aren't careful, you could be in violation. It's okay to hire a virtual assistant to find readers to review books. You must consider how they are getting those reviews. Are they active in Facebook Groups, online forums, or book clubs? Then, you might be okay.

If the virtual assistant is simply exchanging books with other virtual assistants, then that's in clear violation of the policy. You're paying a person to act on your behalf to get fake reviews. It's a no-win situation.

I encourage you to hire a virtual assistant to help manage your self-publishing business if you can afford it. Before you have your assistant gather reviews, make sure you set expectations. Discuss quality control measures to keep good reviews coming in from real readers. You do not want other virtual assistants to post reviews. A sensible way to use a virtual assistant is for community outreach, such as the methods previously mentioned in this book.

Author & Reader Websites

The next type of sites and services are for authors and readers. I encourage you to explore options where websites build a haven for readers to connect with an author. Of course, you have the ARC websites mentioned earlier, but they don't necessarily have a built-in organic reading audience. Those sites merely act as a go-between for authors to get their books to readers. It's entirely up to the author to deliver the traffic.

Author/reader websites will have a clear entry point for authors and readers like Reedsy Discovery. Another example would be a new startup called Pubby.co. Developed and founded by a former CreateSpace employee, Pubby acts as a bridge between author and readers through a unique rewards program. The more a reader participates, the more reward points they receive. Those same rewards points are good for unique opportunities for authors and their readers.

Finding a reputable author and reader website can be tough and require some research. When you're stuck, you can always refer to the Alliance of Independent Authors (ALLi). This company is a non-profit organization based in the UK run by indie authors for indie authors. They spend time researching and curating a list of service providers and websites through their Watchdog Program. When in doubt, cross-check a website or service through their Watchdog Services Directory (DaleLinks.com/Watchdog).

In fact, you can use their free service to investigate all services mentioned in this book. When I can't find a service or website on the list, I'll either pass or request an examination of the services. It's free to submit to ALLi and greatly helps other indie authors make informed decisions.

Editorial Reviews

Suppose you're looking for more premium level reviews from credible sources and authorities in publishing. In that case, editorial reviews are for you. To be clear, you will not get an editorial review posted on Amazon. Editorial reviews are only good for exposure and feedback away from Amazon.

In most editorial review services, you'll get the most detailed analysis of your book. These services focus on your niche, your writing style, any packaging, and even on some book descriptions.

Do not order an editorial review if you don't want to be hyper-analyzed. Since editorial review services commonly work with traditional publishing companies, their readers tend to be more discerning and critical. Where you might have the best editor and proofreader known to man, an editorial reviewer will spot even the slightest transgression in your work.

Since editorial reviews don't appear on Amazon, what function does it serve? Most services have additional perks to showcase the book on their website, email newsletter, or social media. Some services allow the author to choose whether or not their review is public. If the review is less than satisfactory, the author can decline to make the review public.

Since the reviews tend to be so detailed, I'd recommend using the review in other areas on Amazon and beyond. The first place you should post the review is through Amazon Author Central. Simply locate your book, select editorial reviews, and post the review there.

Based on the service provider, Amazon Author Central may limit what you can share. Make sure you read the fine print in advance. For instance, Union Square Review did an editorial review of *Amazon Keywords for Books* (DaleLinks.com/UnionSquareReview). Their request was to share the link to the original review post. That was easy enough!

Though Union Square Review is new to editorial reviews, their reviewers are experienced professionals from all walks of the publishing business.

You may want to take advantage of the well-written editorial review and post it on your website. Just be sure to include a link to your book on Amazon for further context. Also, toss the editorial review in your book, on the cover, or in future editions. It wouldn't hurt to include the editorial review in a press kit when you're trying to land an interview or appearance. When you're reaching out to potential readers for reviews, you can use the editorial review for enticing them to read on. These types of reviews are great for third-party credibility, so take advantage of every opportunity to use it.

The biggest issue when it comes to editorial reviews is the cost. Editorial reviews are not cheap and can range anywhere from $249 to as much as $575. Be selective with who you choose. I included a list of reputable editorial review services in the back of the book. Get editorial reviews if you can afford to do so and have thick skin. Just take heed, an editorial review will not be the ultimate solution to your marketing and promotional needs. Getting the review will not be life-changing. In some instances, an editorial review can be defeating and leave you feeling a little beat up with a little less money. Proceed with caution and only invest in editorial reviews when you can afford it.

*I*n my book *Amazon Keywords for Books*, I touched on the value of getting reviews and building relevance for your title in the Amazon algorithm. Relevance is what Amazon deems as a product's ability to convert a browsing customer into a buyer. To further lend relevance to your book, you can post a comment on every review. This feature is nice and can be a way to build a sense of community around your book.

Be careful when responding to reviews. This road is fraught with dangers and big-time issues. Those who are thin-skinned will never make it to their next book if they aren't careful.

Should an author respond to reviews? Sure. I believe it does show you're actively welcoming feedback. When a reader sees the author took the time to respond to their review, then chances are likely, the reader will:

A. Respond and keep the conversation going

B. Read another book by the author

C. Share their experience about you with other people

After all, it's pretty cool when your favorite author takes the time to read your review, comment on it, and continue the dialogue. In the process, you're simply helping your book by building relevance with the search engine algorithm.

Let's be clear, though, not all reviews are going to be nice. You're not going to like what some people have to say, so how do you respond? Should you respond at all?

To me, it's an all or nothing approach. If you're going to take the time to bask in the glory of a 5-star review, then you need to also humble yourself in the dumpster fire of a 1-star troll. I'd recommend being selective with whether or not you will respond to a review.

If you are going to respond to a review, remember to keep it professional. You might be naturally inclined to pal around with a reader who gave you a great review. That's all well and good, but it tends to send mixed signals when that same reader comes back, dumping on you for a future book. While you stay professional for one, you need to be extra careful with the other. Low reviews are going to have you gritting your teeth and holding back a bit.

Remember, the reviewer did invest in your product, and they have every opportunity to ask for a refund from Amazon. With the liberal thirty-day return policy, a reviewer can and might return your book. Here's the scary thing, the review can remain after the refund.

When it comes to responding to reviews, you'll want to remember a few things:

1. Thank the reviewer first. Remember, they just spent time and money on your book. Those are two valuable commodities you should never take lightly.

2. Be empathetic regardless of the positive or negative tone. It's good to restate key points of feedback in the review.

3. Be brief and share any relevant insights where necessary.

4. Don't get defensive, and don't reject praise. Be grateful.

To further encourage a sense of community, share any interesting reviews with your current readership, social media following, or email list. You'll find it's a great way to prompt other people to leave a review for your book. It's also an indirect way of promoting your book without being overly salesy.

Sharing good reviews works well. If a visitor likes a review, they can click the **Helpful** button below the review. The more customers who click the button, the more the review gets served at the top. This can work for and against you.

If a bad review gets enough helpful votes, it'll be the first thing browsing customers see on a page. That can work against you.

Whatever you do, don't send traffic, and coerce them to hit the **Helpful** button. You can bring attention to the feature, but don't manipulate the results simply to drive up your favorite review. As an example, you could send out an email with this call-to-action:

> "This book is the best book that has ever been written! 5 stars!" Amazon Reviewer
>
> What do you think about that review? Would you agree with it? If someone hasn't read my book, do you think it would be helpful or not? Check out the full review at (insert the review link here)...

You'll notice I didn't guide my email subscriber into doing one action or the other. I simply shared the review, asked for insights, and directed my subscribers to check out the review for themselves on Amazon. Don't forget to insert the link to the review. Most people will not bother checking out a review if there isn't a link.

> Bonus Tip: Insert a screenshot of the review. It tends to help with finding the review once your follower visits the product review page.

Whoops, This Review Doesn't Belong Here

Yep, it happens. Some ding-dong posted a review for a completely different product altogether. We're not entirely sure how it got there, but it did happen.

Then, some reviewers post a review despite never reading or buying the product. They'll even fully disclose they never purchased or read the book.

The last types of reviews are predatory or targeted harassment. Sadly, these types of reviews are nearly impossible to remove. You have to prove the reader is maliciously posting reviews on your products to drive away buyers or slow down sales. I tried disputing several predatory reviewers, but Amazon wouldn't hear of it. They feel it's important to allow all reviewers to post both positive and negative feedback. Anything short of a signed confession will not work to take the review down. Simply take it on the chin and move along.

If you begin to see a pattern of abuse, you can always contact Amazon and highlight the issues. However, don't hold your breath on the problem getting resolved. You can at least breathe a sigh of relief in knowing bad actors eventually hang themselves with their own rope. I found many predatory reviews eventually disappear along with the Amazon reviewer profile. When Amazon detects suspicious activity, they'll put that fire out in due time, especially with consistent and clear abuse of their community guidelines.

Also of note, Amazon is now allowing review ratings without representation. Essentially, readers can leave a star rating and do not have to justify it. This new feature can be good, but it can also be confusing for authors. Without knowing why someone rated a book a certain way, it's hard to adjust the publication. Of course, it's impossible to remove review ratings since no one knows who rated it and why.

Can You Share Amazon Reviews Elsewhere?

Amazon is protective of its trademark and property. Part of their property includes the reviews posted on their platform. Sadly, no clear guideline or rule states whether or not you can share their property on other sites. To err on the side of caution, share short snippets for reviews from Amazon when you do. It can fall under fair use, and you are somewhat safe.

> Fair use is a doctrine in the United States law permitting limited use of copyrighted content without having permission from the copyright holder.[8]

Be careful, though. Fair use isn't something you can abuse or have to protect you if you draw Amazon's ire. In my experience, I never heard of Amazon sending a DMCA takedown notice for sharing their reviews on a website, social media, through an email, or anywhere else.

I used to encourage authors to post a review through Amazon Author Central in the editorial reviews section. However, this creates redundancy on your product page and doesn't do anything but create more stuff for browsing customers to read. If you don't have an editorial review or reviews posted from other areas to share in the editorial reviews section, leave it blank.

O n Amazon, you have the hidden option to make an ebook permanently free. Even though Kindle Direct Publishing (KDP) will not allow you to price an ebook below ninety-nine cents, you can price it as free with a few extra steps. Publish your ebook through Kindle Direct Publishing but avoid opting into the KDP Select program. Then, publish your title on other sites like Apple, Barnes & Noble, Kobo, or Google Play Books where you can publish your title for free.

Once your title is available through the other sites, contact KDP through your dashboard and request a price match for your title. For a deeper dive into how and why you should publish a permafree book, be sure to check out my short guide, *Secrets of the Permafree Book* (DaleLinks.com/PermafreeBook).

Even **Secrets of the Permafree Book** is set as permanently free in this example. It's a great way to garner more reviews and build brand awareness.

Once you make your title free, promote it just like you would any other book. You'll be amazed at how many more reviews you'll get organically. Why? It's free!

In 2015, my mentor challenged me to produce eight to ten short books for my fitness niche. He wanted me to publish the ebooks as permafree. It just so happened I was sitting on a few short reads already, so it wasn't a tall task. Once I published the books, I saw a huge increase in sales for my normally priced books. Also, there was an additional uptick in organic reviews, especially on the permafree books.

Fast forward to about 2018, and those same permafree books had a decent amount of reviews. Sadly, I didn't see as many downloads, and not as many buyers were going to the full-priced books. I switched the permafree books into fully paid books. The nice part was I didn't have to do any review gathering. People naturally left reviews over the three years since I published them.

Before you dive into this methodology, you need to be aware it comes with its share of heartaches. When you allow readers to download your ebooks for free, quite a few people will do so and feel entitled to beat up the publication. I discussed this issue with several other authors in other niches. They expressed the same. Whenever a book is free, a different subset of hyper-critical readers grab a copy and leave a bad review. It's not to say the free book readers ruined my book with bad reviews, but you certainly see lower reviews across the board.

This may have a lot to do with the perceived value. If a customer sees an item is free, they'll value it far less than a full-priced book. We could even theorize those lacking the funds typically have a different mindset than those who can afford full-priced books. So, their expectations are going to be a bit more grandiose.

Nonetheless, if you want to get more organic reviews, one of the easiest ways is to make your ebook free. Then, promote the heck out of the book to get more downloads. Once you get so many downloads, you can expect to see more organic reviews.

O ne of the biggest missed opportunities right now in self-publishing is in audiobooks. If you do not have your work published in audiobooks, then you must not skip this chapter. You'll discover why getting reviews through audiobooks is even easier than print and ebook. To make matters better, Amazon equips you with all you need to get more reviews on your books.

When you publish your audiobook exclusively through the Amazon-owned Audiobook Creation Exchange (ACX), you get up to 100 promotional codes per audiobook. These codes are a great way to gift copies for the audiobook marketplace, Audible. In turn, your readers – or in this case, listeners – will hopefully leave a review.

In years past, ACX had a glaring hole in their system where promotional codes were good for any audiobook on Audible. In early 2020, ACX closed up the loophole. Now, promotional codes are only good for a given audiobook while carrying no monetary value.

Think of the Audible promo codes as a way to build an ARC team for your audiobooks. Sadly, since ACX doesn't have a pre-order feature at this time, it's technically not an advanced copy. That's okay because the result is the same.

Follow the same best practices when it comes to soliciting reviews. You can reach out to your current readership, influencers, bloggers,

YouTubers, and beyond. Nothing is off-limits when it comes to getting reviews on the Audible platform, and that's where the issue lies.

The listeners will download and listen to your audiobook. Then, they can leave a review on Audible, not Amazon. Can the listener leave an unverified purchase review on Amazon? Sure! You can even recommend it once they've posted a review on Audible. For now, there's no integration between Audible to Amazon with the reviews. It's the opposite for the other way around.

On Audible, browsing customers can see the reviews posted on Amazon for the book under a special tab next to the Audible Reviews. Having the Amazon reviews integrated on Audible is a plus. It would just be nice to see it reciprocated on the Amazon platform for Audible reviews. Then, product listings would get even more reviews to build social proof.

I believe Amazon and Audible will eventually integrate both ways. Not too long ago, Amazon allowed for cross-region propagation of reviews. Previously, you could only see U.S. reviews in the U.S. and U.K. reviews in the U.K. Now, see all the reviews across every region on most Amazon sites. Amazon does take a while to post the reviews across all sites, but they are showing up eventually.

Since Amazon is always changing, tweaking, and evolving their website for a better customer experience, I imagine we'll see an Audible and Amazon integration. You can then see more than just two product review types – in ebook, print books, and audiobooks.

Other Audiobook Promo Codes

Another platform to publish your audiobook is Findaway Voices. This audiobook publishing platform distributes to over forty different audiobook retail sites and libraries. When you publish through Findaway Voices, you get thirty promotional codes good for the Author's Direct audiobook platform. If you publish exclusively through Findaway Voices, then you get 100 promotional codes.

The idea works the same way as Audible promo codes do. You send the promo code, and the listener gets a free download of your audiobook. The listener can then leave a review on their preferred audiobook platform. In theory, your listener could post an unverified purchase review of your audiobook on Amazon.

If you want wider distribution beyond what ACX offers, then you may want to consider Findaway Voices. The only catch is you must agree to be non-exclusive on ACX. You then get smaller royalties (25% non-exclusive versus 40% exclusive). Findaway Voices realized the predicament of losing the Audible promotional codes and, in turn, made up for it through their promo code system.

Audiobook Promo Code Sites & Facebook Groups

Much like getting reviews for your print books and ebooks, you can get readers through various websites and services. Focus on the author and reader websites first. Some services will cost you. For instance, AudiobookBoom.com has a premium service where you can advertise your audiobook promotional codes through their email newsletter or website. When listeners are interested in getting a promo code, Audiobook Boom will send you an email notification with all the pertinent contact information.

One of the best resources yet is Facebook Groups. Simply visit Facebook, search "audiobook promo codes" or "free audiobooks," and you'll get many groups devoted to connecting listeners with authors. This is, by far, the best free resource for getting reviews.

The one advantage audiobooks have over print and ebooks is accessibility. It's much easier to listen to an audiobook than to sit down and read it yourself. You can listen to an audiobook in almost any situation and adjust the reading speed to blaze through the content quicker. Once you publish an audiobook, I highly recommend getting those promotional codes out to as many listeners as possible who are willing to post a review after listening.

had a book once that got a one-star review right after publishing. The low review crushed me! The reviewer clearly had a bias against the topic. In no way was he willing to read or learn more about the content. They planned to push their opposing viewpoint. In a panic, I tried my best to get reviews. Since the topic was a rather niche subject, finding reviewers wasn't going to be easy.

Despite the low review, the sales kept coming in. After a while, I abandoned the search for more reviews while focusing on higher priorities. While I managed other tasks, I had Amazon ads sending traffic to the one-star rated book. Oddly enough, customers still bought the book. Slowly, more positive reviews rolled in and buried the negative review. During the time between, the book continued to get consistent sales.

Can reviews really make or break the success of a book? Well, this depends largely on what you do with them. I mentioned how you could reframe negative reviews in a way that draws in more positive reviews. I even shared how you can share positive reviews to get more engagement on your product page. I explained how commenting helps build a sense of community around your book.

Suppose you simply roll over and expect Amazon to dish out buying customers who'll also post a review. In that case, you're going to be in for a rude awakening. You must put in the effort to see some type of return. Having a book published on Amazon isn't enough to get sales or gather reviews. You need to have a consistent action plan that includes gathering reviews for your books.

Will you always get reviews from every reader? No, but you greatly increase your odds of winning if you play the game. You cannot play the game with your hands in your pockets or through inconsistent practices. Know where you're going, how you're getting there, and what you need to do to improve your results.

Also, it's not good enough for you to simply gather reviews and call it a day. You need to read the reviews and take notes. Your readers tell you what they like best about your book and what needs to change about it. Before you do make any changes, it's a good idea to take it all with a grain of salt.

One adage holds true when it comes to reviews:

> If one person calls you an ass, ignore them. If five people call you an ass, buy a saddle.

One review might not be enough to draw a conclusion. You may need numerous reviews saying the same thing before you consider adjusting your publication. How many reviews are enough to draw statistical significance? That's going to be up to you.

My book, *The Home Workout Plan for Seniors*, is a prime example of an egregious oversight on my part. In concept, the content made sense, but in practice, I failed. When I launched the book, I had a handful of happy reviews. Then, I noticed a few trickling in from the U.K. They were not happy with the content and for a good reason.

My big oversight was in how I formatted the content for the audience. Since senior citizens would read the content, it would've been in my best interests to make the print large and the pictures even larger still. Sadly, I formatted the content like any other book, and I paid dearly in the reviews.

For whatever reason, life called me away from my fitness books, and I never found the time to update the content. When I finally did get around to fixing the interior, the reviews were brutal. A majority of the reviews complained about the small print and smaller pictures. They had every right to complain, and I had to take it on the chin. Rather than roll over, I course-corrected, updated the content, and kept the low reviews.

Quite a few readers were unhappy, and I listened to their requests. Now, the book continues to sell a few copies here and there. Will it ever recover from the pounding it took from the reviews? Time will tell. Maybe I need to take a bit of my own advice and slap a few more reviews on the book now that it's updated.

Getting reviews isn't difficult, but it isn't so easy you can sit back and just have them rain down from nowhere. While selling books alone is difficult, you can certainly lighten the burden by getting a bit of social proof through reviews. Can reviews make or break the success of your book? That's entirely up to what you do about it. What will *you* do?

*A*fter the first time I visited Condado Tacos, I waddled out of the restaurant and immediately fumbled for my phone. My first inclination was to leave a detailed review because I didn't want anyone else to miss out on the same experience I enjoyed. It would also commemorate the great time I had throwing down more tacos than my stomach should ever handle at any one time. Indirectly, I helped build just a little credibility for this small restaurant tucked below a luxury apartment building in the heart of downtown Columbus.

Could Condado Tacos exist or even thrive without my review or the countless others left online? Sure, but it'd be that much harder to drive traffic into their establishment. They most likely would have to spend a ton of money on marketing and promotion through mail-out ads or commercials on the radio. Why waste money on it? Customer reviews are the best type of advertising, and they're free!

If you're ever at an impasse, and you're wondering if anyone will ever buy your book, you need to take a hard look at your review gathering process. Once you start getting reviews, it's important to keep the traffic coming to your book and build awareness about the value of leaving a review of your book. Also, never stop asking for reviews. When you do get reviews, show enough self-awareness to adjust your book to suit the readers. That way, you aren't blindly pushing forward to the detriment of your book. As some people say, "Don't cut off your nose to spite your face."

Much like Condado Tacos or any other company, service, or product, it's going to take time to build trust in the public eye. Focus on your long game. It's going to be awhile to amass enough social proof to gain random strangers' trust. That's what getting reviews is all about – getting enough validation from an outside party that merits other people trying you out too.

When you get beat up by a low-star review or some disparaging words, remember even the best books, brands, and companies have dealt with it before. Once you've hit that point, remind yourself you've made it! Everyone from JK Rowling to Charles Dickens to Stephen King to Tony Robbins has low reviews. Never throw the towel in if you get beat up a little in the reviews.

As we wrap up this book about getting reviews, I want to leave you with a final thought. Getting reviews is an integral part of any marketing and promotional plan. Marketing and promotion are a never-ending task. It's not like you can publish your book on Amazon, run a few ad campaigns, and then call it a day. Suppose you want long term, sustainable earnings from your books. In that case, you'll have to devote most of your energy and resources to marketing and promotion. Part of that promotional strategy should be getting reviews. As you discovered from this book, it doesn't have to cost a dime most of the time. When it does, you need to measure the effectiveness before ever trying it again.

One last thing before you go out there and get your book reviews—it's not enough you learn the best practices for getting book reviews. You must implement the knowledge. Simply reading a book about getting reviews is not going to give you reviews alone. Much like getting a gym membership, you actually have to do the work to reap the results. Once you do kick into action and start getting reviews, reward yourself with a tasty taco. You deserve it!

Now that you finished reading this book, what did you think of what you read? Were there any tips or information you found insightful? What do you think was missing from this book? While you're thinking back on what you read, it'd mean the world to me if you left an honest review on Amazon.

As you learned, reviews play a part in building relevance for all products on Amazon. So, whether you found the information helpful or not, your candid review would help other customers make an informed purchase.

Also, based on your review, I'll adjust this publication and future editions. That way, you and other indie authors can learn and grow.

Feel free to leave a review at DaleLinks.com/ReviewReviewsBook.

Dale L. Roberts is a self-publishing advocate, award-winning author, and video content creator. Dale's inherent passion for life fuels his self-publishing advocacy both in print and online. After publishing over 40 titles and becoming an international bestselling author on Amazon, Dale started his YouTube channel, *Self-Publishing with Dale*. Voted by Feedspot among the Top 50 YouTube channels about self-publishing, Dale cemented his position as the indie-author community's go-to authority.

Dale currently lives with his wife Kelli and cat Izzie in Columbus, Ohio.

Relevant links:

- Website – SelfPublishingWithDale.com

- YouTube – YouTube.com/SelfPublishingWithDale

- Twitter – Twitter.com/SelfPubWithDale

- Facebook – Facebook.com/SelfPubWithDale

- Instagram – Instagram.com/SelfPubWithDale

- DON'T GO HERE! – DaleLinks.com

Become a Keyword Master and Watch Your Book Sales Grow

If you can master keywords, then you can master your book's success! Dale L. Roberts is here to help you do that! In Amazon Keywords for Books, Dale shows you how to use keywords to sell more books. It's not difficult to increase the discoverability of your book. But you'll need a deeper understanding of keywords if you want to sell more books.

If you're ready to learn more and sell more through keyword mastery, then get your copy of *Amazon Keywords for Books* at…

DaleLinks.com/KeywordsBook

Unlock the Secrets to Exploding Your Author Brand through Marketing & Promotion

Get real-world practical advice you can use for marketing and promoting your book and author brand. Dale L. Roberts shines the light on many methods for aspiring authors to sell more books. The best part of marketing and promotion is you don't need to have a ton of money or time to make it work. Dale will show you how to spend less and earn more through book sales.

When you're ready to take action and learn more, grab your copy of *Promotional Strategies for Books* at…

DaleLinks.com/PromoBook

Pivoting my author brand from fitness to self-publishing has been a long time in the making. I started writing and publishing back in 2013, went into the business full-time in late 2014, and started gaining real traction in 2016. My last published fitness book was in late 2016, and that's when I started focusing on *Self-Publishing with Dale* on YouTube. It took roughly four years for me to produce a book about self-publishing at last. It wouldn't have happened without the love and support of many wonderful people.

If you know or follow any of my content, you know I have the unwavering support and loyalty of my wife, Kelli. I owe so much to her and where I am today. I don't think I was ready to assume this much responsibility back in 2013. She challenged me every step of the way while ensuring I had the support system not to let failure hold me back. No one has a wife quite like mine. No one.

Ava Fails is, in large part, the reason why I'm able to accomplish as much as I do. She's smart, honest, and loyal. It's hard to believe she's been working with me for over four years now. What?! When my fitness brand was flying high, Ava was there. Even in its dying days, Ava was there. When we transitioned to focusing on *Self-Publishing with Dale*, Ava was there. Even when I couldn't afford to hire her, Ava still stuck around. I'm forever grateful for your loyalty, services, and friendship. You're the best.

A big thank you to the team at Archangel Ink for enduring my constant demands over the past five publications. Folks, if you happen to read the special thanks, you must know Archangel Ink has amazing services dedicated to self-publishers who need a little extra help. It just so happens I hired them to do my book interiors and the cover for my book Secrets of the Permafree Book. If you're struggling to put it all together, I highly recommend working with Archangel Ink. Please accept my virtual banana sticker for all your hard work, Archangel Ink.

Though these special thanks seem like a rehash of my previous three books, I do take the time to express how much I truly appreciate everyone in a meaningful way. However, I don't want to make my content only about thanking people. I'd like to thank: Dan Norton, Rob Archangel, Walt Roberts, Kevin Maguire, Keith Wheeler, Mojo Siedlak, Dave Chesson, Julie Broad of Book Launchers, Scott Jay Marshall II, Jason Stallworth, Jason Bracht, Russ Webster, Harold Webb, my mother Kaye Cox, Vicki Haas, Saketh Kumar, pip-squeaky, John Fitch, John Waaser, Jacob Rothenberg, Chandler Bolt, Hannah & Jay Jacobson at Book Award Pro, Jason Jones at PR Toolkit, William Mays, Omanah Bultman, Brittany Putzer, Lafiro Gomez III, Kyle Atkinson, and many more.

Thank you to all of my video content creator family. They include Nick Nimmin, Brian G Johnson, Dan Currier, Andrew Kan, Eddie Garrison, Doug Hewson, Regor Onafetsid, Derral Eves, Jeremy Vest, Roberto Blake, Shannon Vlogs, Evan & Nina Carmichael, Helen Kinson, Christina Sisson, and so many more.

If I missed your name, my apologies. Don't take it as a sign of being ungrateful. It's more that I don't have the best memory and try my best to remember everyone I can.

Oh, and how could I forget – Condado Tacos on 132 S. High St. in Columbus, Ohio. I've easily spent thousands eating there. Why? The atmosphere gets my creative juices flowing. I love to use it as a reward or for talking business with other peers in my industry. Big thank you to Lincoln, Lili, Devin, and the rest of the staff! Also, a shout out to the former-Condado server, Wade. We miss you, man! You all make life so much fun with premium tacos. I promise I'm not getting paid to write this. I legitimately love Condado Tacos.

- The Alliance of Independent Authors (ALLi) Watchdog Services - https://selfpublishingadvice.org/best-self-publishing-services/
- Hidden Gems Books The Good and Bad of Amazon's $50 Review Rule - https://www.hiddengemsbooks.com/amazons-50-review-rule/
- Kindlepreneur: HOW TO GET FREE BOOK REVIEWS WITH NO BLOG, NO LIST, AND NO BEGGING - https://kindlepreneur.com/how-to-get-book-reviews-with-no-blog-no-list-and-no-begging/
- Reedsy
  - > Best Book Review Blogs of 2020 - https://blog.reedsy.com/book-review-blogs/
  - > The Best Book Review Sites For Enthusiastic Readers - https://reedsy.com/discovery/blog/book-review-sites
  - > Reedsy Discovery - https://reedsy.com/discovery/submit

Review Sites & Services

- Book Blogger List - https://bookbloggerlist.com/
- Book Reviewer Yellow Pages - https://bookrevieweryellowpages.com/book-bloggers/
- Digital Pubbing - https://digitalpubbing.com/7-strategies-and-94-tools-to-help-indie-authors-find-readers-and-reviewers/
- Kate McKillan's Outbox Online Design Studio - https://www.outboxonline.com/book-review-submission/

- Library Journal - https://www.libraryjournal.com/?page=Review-Submissions
- Library Thing - https://www.librarything.com/
- Self-Publishing Review - https://www.selfpublishingreview.com/spr-bestseller-book-packages/
- The Indie View - http://www.theindieview.com/indie-reviewers/
- Triskele Books - http://triskelebooks.blogspot.com/2013/03/indie-friendly-book-reviewers.html
- Tweet Your Books - https://www.tweetyourbooks.com/p/free-reviews.html
- Writing World - https://www.tweetyourbooks.com/p/free-reviews.html

Editorial Reviews

- Foreword Reviews - https://publishers.forewordreviews.com/reviews/
- Clarion Reviews - https://publishers.forewordreviews.com/reviews/#service-clarion-review
- Kirkus Reviews - https://www.kirkusreviews.com/indie-reviews/
- Union Square Reviews - https://unionsquarereview.com/
- Independent Book Review - https://www.selfpublishingreview.com/spr-bestseller-book-packages/
- NetGalley - https://www.netgalley.com/

Audiobook Promo Code Sites

- Audiobook Boom – https://audiobookboom.com/authors
- Audiofreebies - https://www.audiofreebies.com/add-an-audiobook/
- Audiobooks Unleashed - https://audiobooksunleashed.com/add-an-audiobook/
- Free Audiobook Codes - https://freeaudiobookcodes.com/advertisers/

Reviews ▾ **References** 🔍

1   Collinger, T. (n.d.) How Online Reviews Influence Sales. https://spiegel.medill.northwestern.edu/online-reviews/.

2   Amazon.com LLC. (n.d.) Community Guidelines. https://www.amazon.com/gp/help/customer/display.html.

3   Amazon.com LLC. (n.d.) About Amazon Verified Purchase Reviews. https://www.amazon.com/gp/help/customer/display.html?nodeId=202076110.

4   Cooper. D. (24 July 2015). Amazon accused of spying on reviewer's social media profiles. https://www.engadget.com/2015-07-24-amazon-social-media-ebook-review-relationship-imy-santiago.html.

5   Chesson, D. (8 February 2019) THE ULTIMATE GUIDE TO GOODREADS FOR AUTHORS. https://kindlepreneur.com/how-to-use-goodreads-for-authors/#anchor-2.

6   Gaughran, D. (2 June 2018) When #Cockygate And #Tiffanygate Collide. https://davidgaughran.com/2018/06/02/cockygate-faleena-hopkins-tiffanygate-chance-carter/.

7   Rutkowska, A. (n.d.) BOOK LAUNCH REVIEWS: LAUNCHING WITH 100+ REVIEWS. https://kindlepreneur.com/book-launch-reviews-launching-with-100-reviews/

8   Library of Congress. (n.d.) More Information on Fair Use. https://copyright.gov/fair-use/more-info.html.

Made in the USA
Monee, IL
20 January 2023